4th Grade Suggested Reading List

Adler, David
Cam Jansen: And the Mystery of the Television Dog

Ackerman, Karen
The Night Crossing

Barrett, Judi
Cloudy with a Chance of Meatballs

Catling, Patrick Skene
The Chocolate Touch

Christian, Mary Blount
Sebastian (Super Sleuth) and the Copycat Crime

Clifford, Eth
Flatfoot Fox and the Case of the Missing Whoooo

Dalgliesh, Alice
Courage of Sarah Noble

Delton, Judy
Angel Bites the Bullet

Demuth, Patricia
Brennan in Trouble with Teacher

DePaola, Tomie
Legend of the Bluebonnet

Dorros, Arthur
Abuela

Ernst, Lisa Campbell
Nattie Parson's Good Luck Lamb

Fox, Paula
Maurice's Room

Gleiter, Jan
Paul Revere

Graff, Stewart
Helen Keller: Toward the Light

Jeschke, Susan
Perfect the Pig

Jones, Charlotte
Accidents May Happen: Fifty Inventions Discovered by Mistake

Kellogg, Steven
Paul Bunyan

Korman, Gordon
No Coins, Please

Kroll, Steven
Andrew Wants a Dog

Lindgren, Astrid
Pippi Goes on Board

Manes, Stephen
Be a Perfect Person in Just Three Days

McArthur, Nancy
The Plant That Ate Dirty Socks

McDonald, Megan
Judy Moody Gets Famous

McMullan, Kate
Dinosaur Hunters

O'Connor, Jim
Jackie Robinson and the Story of All-Black Baseball

Raskin, Ellen
Nothing Ever Happens on My Block

Rowling, J. K.
Harry Potter Series

Schroeder, Alan
A Story of Young Harriet Tubman

Smith, Janet Lee
The Monster in the Third Dresser Drawer
It's Not Easy Being George

Smith, Robert Kimmer
Chocolate Fever

Sobol, Donald J.
Encyclopedia Brown Series

Stadler, John
Animal Cafe

Stock, Catherine
Emma's Dragon Hunt

Stoutenburg, Adrien
American Tall Tales

Waber, Bernard
Lyle, Lyle, Crocodile

Walter, Mildred Pitts
Justin and the Best Biscuits in the World

Whelan, Gloria
Next Spring an Oriole

What's That Noise?

Going camping sounded fun to Jenny, except for one thing—bears. Jenny was afraid of them. She had heard that a lot of bears lived in Yellowstone National Park, and that is exactly where her family was going.

After setting up their tent, Jenny and her family ate dinner. Soon the light of day turned into night's darkness. Jenny helped clean up around camp; then her father locked all their food in the car.

"There, now. That will keep the bears away from our food," he said.

Jenny shivered. "I hope they'll leave us alone too."

"They will," her mother reassured her calmly.

After climbing into their sleeping bags, everyone fell asleep, except Jenny. She lay awake listening to all the sounds around her. Her father snored while crickets chirped. All of a sudden, a rustling sound erupted outside the tent. Jenny's heart pounded, and her breathing quickened. She was too petrified to speak. Finally she couldn't stand it anymore.

"Dad."

"Huh?" her Dad mumbled.

"There's a bear outside."

Her dad listened. The rustling sound grew louder.

"Let's see." He crawled over to the window. Jenny couldn't believe how brave he was.

Her father laughed. "Would you like to see your bear?"

Cautiously, Jenny made her way over to the window. She looked out to where two raccoons were sniffing around a clump of bushes.

Jenny took a deep breath and relaxed. "At least it wasn't a bear ... this time."

2

About
Skill Builders
Reading

by Bettyanne Gillette

Welcome to Rainbow Bridge Publishing's Skill Builders series. Like our Summer Bridge Activities™ collection, the Skill Builders series is designed to make learning both fun and rewarding.

Skill Builders Reading offers a variety of writing types to engage and challenge grade-four readers. Reading material is grade-level appropriate, and the exercises help students master important reading and comprehension skills, including main idea, sequence, details, predicting outcomes and vocabulary.

This workbook will hold students' interest with a mix of humor, imagination and instruction as they steadily improve their reading comprehension and other skills. The diverse assignments enhance reading skills while giving students something fun to think about—from Mozart to movies.

A critical thinking section is included to help students move beyond comprehension and develop higher-order thinking skills.

Learning is more effective when approached with an element of fun and enthusiasm—just as most children approach life. That's why the Skill Builders combine entertaining and academically sound exercises with eye-catching graphics and fun themes—to make reviewing basic skills at school or home fun and effective, for both you and your budding scholars.

Table of Contents

1. Write *F* for fact or *O* for opinion in the blank next to each sentence.
   A. ___ Camping is not fun at all.
   B. ___ Her father snored while crickets chirped.
   C. ___ Jenny made her way over to the window.
   D. ___ Seeing a bear would be scary.

2. Write *S* for same or *D* for different in the blank next to each sentence.
   A. ___ Bears have claws. Horses have hooves.
   B. ___ Jenny was afraid. Her dad wasn't.
   C. ___ Jenny's mom and dad went to sleep. Jenny didn't.
   D. ___ light of day, night's darkness

3. Circle the correct answer.
   A. A lot of bears live in _____.
      a park   Yellowstone Park   Central Park

   B. Jenny looked out the _____.
      window   door   hole in the tent

   C. Two raccoons sniffed around some _____.
      flowers   trees   bushes

   D. Jenny's family hoped the bears wouldn't bother their
      _____.
      clothes   shoes   food

4. Bonus Word Play
   Homophones are words that have the same sound but are spelled differently. Find the right homophone for each word in the story.
   sea _____
   there _____
   eight _____

The Faces of Mount Rushmore

Mount Rushmore is located in the Black Hills of South Dakota. It stands 6,000 feet tall, and the faces of four U.S. presidents are carved into its side: George Washington, Thomas Jefferson, Theodore Roosevelt, and Abraham Lincoln. Each face is as tall as a five-story building.

Gutzon Borglum was sixty years old when he started to sculpt the mountain. He led a crew of 400 workers. It took them fourteen years to complete the faces. They actually spent only six years working on the mountain. The other eight years were lost because of bad weather or lack of money.

Borglum's crew used dynamite to blast granite from the mountain. Then they used special tools to make each face as smooth as a sidewalk. By the end of the project, 450,000 tons of granite had been removed. Amazingly, only a few people were hurt during the work.

The mountain was named after Charles E. Rushmore, a lawyer from New York. Rushmore was famous for helping people who had mines in South Dakota in the 1800s.

Gutzon Borglum passed away in 1941. He died before the carving of Mount Rushmore was finished. His son, Lincoln, finished the work.

Before Borglum died, someone asked him how long the faces on Mount Rushmore would remain. He said, "Until the wind and the rain alone shall wear them away."

Reading Comprehension

1. Underline the cause, and circle the effect.
   A. Four hundred people carved the mountain. Millions visit Mount Rushmore each year.
   B. Dynamite was used. Four hundred fifty thousand tons of granite were removed.
   C. Gutzon Borglum passed away. His son finished the job for him.
   D. Special tools were used. Each face is as smooth as a sidewalk.

2. Crossword Puzzle

   Across
   3. These were used to make the faces smooth.
   5. This was used to blast the granite.
   6. The faces on the mountain and sidewalks are both _____.

   Down
   1. one of the presidents on Mount Rushmore
   2. one of the presidents on Mount Rushmore
   4. Four of these were carved on the mountain.

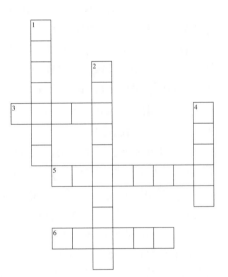

3. Number the events in the order they occurred in the story.
   A. ___ The mountain was named after Charles E. Rushmore.
   B. ___ Six years were spent working on the mountain.
   C. ___ Dynamite was used to blast the granite.
   D. ___ Only a few people were hurt.

4. Bonus Word Play
   How many syllables are in each word?
   Rushmore ____   Presidents ____   Washington____

5

Professional Football

Some people say football began in Greece a long time ago. The game was called *harpston*. Any number of people could play. The players would kick, throw, or run a ball across a goal line.

Football came to America in the late 1800s. Football combined two English sports: soccer and rugby. Football became so popular in England that the leaders of the country forbade the people from playing the sport. They didn't want it to distract people from the military sport of archery.

Hacking used to be part of the game of football. Hacking was when a player kicked another player in the shins to get him to drop the ball. Some people thought hacking was dangerous. Others thought hacking was a good idea. Because the people couldn't agree, one of the first football leagues was formed. The league wanted to make the rules the same for everyone. As a result, hacking was dropped from the game.

You play football on a field that is 100 yards long. At each end of the field is a goalpost. Carrying the ball over the goal line or kicking the ball through the goalposts scores points. This is similar to rugby.

Football is one of America's favorite pastimes. Every year, nearly one billion people all over the world watch the Super Bowl. People especially like the Super Bowl commercials. Because the Super Bowl is so popular, buying advertising time is expensive. A thirty-second commercial can cost 2.3 million dollars.

1. Write *T* for true or *F* for false in the blank next to each sentence.
   A. ___ Football has become one of America's least favorite pastimes.
   B. ___ Everyone thought hacking was a good idea.
   C. ___ A thirty-second Super Bowl commercial can cost 2.3 million dollars.
   D. ___ Football began as a result of combining two sports: rugby and soccer.

2. Fill in the blank with the right word from the story.
   A. A game called _____ was once played in Greece.
   B. Billions of people all over the world watch the

   _____ _____.

   C. Football has fast become one of America's favorite

   _____.

   D. In England, football was forbidden because it took away from the sport of _____.

3. Match the sentence with the correct answer in the box.
   A. A football field is _____.
   B. Some people thought hacking was

   _____.

   C. Players score points by kicking the ball through the _____.
   D. During the Super Bowl, people like watching the _____.

   > 1. dangerous
   > 2. commercials
   > 3. 100 yards long
   > 4. goal posts

4. Bonus Word Play
   Unscramble the following word: S   N   L   I   I   M   L   O

   _____

   _____

Hilary sat up at the sound of the buzzer going off in the kitchen.

"The cake's finished," she said to her best friend, Jen, who was sitting on the floor painting her toenails. Hilary ran to the kitchen to take the cake out of the oven. Then she went back to the bedroom to get Jen.

"Come help me decorate it," Hilary said.

Jen looked up. "You have to wait for it to cool first," she said. Hilary flopped on the bed and watched while Jen stroked the purple polish over her nails. Hilary rolled onto her back and leafed through a magazine. Finally she gave up.

"Let's go see if it's ready," she said, dragging Jen up by the arm. "Kim's birthday will be over by the time we get the cake frosted."

On the counter in the kitchen sat a rectangular-shaped chocolate cake. Hilary put her hand on top of it. "It feels cool," she said. Jen placed her hand next to Hilary's. She frowned.

"I don't know," Jen said. "It feels kind of warm to me."

"It'll be okay," Hilary said. "Frosting sticks to everything."

Hilary opened a can of white frosting, and they took turns spreading frosting across the cake.

"This is harder than I thought," Hilary said.

"Yeah, the cake keeps sticking to the frosting," added Jen.

"Maybe the crumbs won't show when we write on it," Hilary said. She opened a tube of pink frosting.

"I hope so," Jen said, tasting some frosting from the tube.

Hilary tried writing *Happy*. Then Jen tried writing *Birthday*. When they were through, the cake was still so warm that their words melted into a glob of pink frosting with lots of crumbs mixed in.

"This doesn't look good," Hilary said.

"Yeah, but I'll bet it tastes good," said Jen.

"I've got an idea," Hilary said and bolted back upstairs to her room.

A half hour later, Hilary and Jen stood on Kim's doorstep with a freckled cake and a scarf to use as a blindfold.

1. Write *F* for fact or *O* for opinion in the blank next to each sentence.
A. ___ Hilary and Jen decorated a cake for Kim.
B. ___ Frosting a cake is hard.
C. ___ Hilary and Jen should be proud of themselves.
D. ___ Hilary and Jen brought a blindfold to Kim's house.

2. Write *S* for same or *D* for different in the blank next to each sentence.
A. ___ Hilary and Jen thought decorating a cake was hard.
B. ___ Hilary and Jen liked cake decorating.
C. ___ Hilary and Jen disagreed about whether or not the cake was cool enough.
D. ___ Hilary wrote, and then Jen wrote, on the birthday cake.

3. Circle the right answer.
A. Because they wanted to give Kim a birthday cake, Hilary and Jen were _____.
grumpy   general   generous
B. Jen thought the cake was too _____ to frost.
good   warm   expensive
C. Jen and Hilary thought the cake would taste _____.
good   bad   stale

4. Bonus Word Play
Antonyms are words that have opposite meanings. Find the antonym in the story for each of the following words:
closed _____
off_____
bottom _____
cool _____

The International Space Station

The Soviet Union sent the first space station into orbit in 1971. It was called *Salyut 1*. The first crew sent to visit the station couldn't get inside because the hatch wouldn't work. The next crew got in and stayed for 24 days. However, a valve in their capsule broke as they were returning to Earth. The air escaped, and all three members of the crew were killed.

The Russians launched a second space station in 1973. This station had problems while it was in orbit, and no one ever lived on it. During this time, the United States launched its first space station. It was called *Skylab*. The first crew stayed in space for 28 days. The last *Skylab* crew stayed for 84 days. *Skylab* was no longer used after 1974.

The Russians and Americans learned many things from their space stations. For example, after a long stay, astronauts were so weak when they returned to Earth that they couldn't stand up. As a result, exercise equipment was put on space stations.

In 1986 the Soviets launched another space station. This space station was called *Mir*, which means "peace" in Russian. *Mir* was different from other space stations. It was designed so that parts could be added on to it. Rockets could dock with the station to bring more supplies and fuel. In 1995 an American astronaut visited *Mir* and lived there for three months. The record for the longest time in space was set on *Mir*, too—438 days.

In 1998 the first section of the new International Space Station was sent into orbit. In November of 2000, a crew arrived at their new home over 200 miles above the earth to start a new chapter in space station history.

1. Underline the cause, and circle the effect.

A. The first crew didn't enter the space station. The hatch was broken.

B. The second crew died. A valve was broken.

C. The men were too weak to stand. Exercise equipment was put on the next space station.

D. The *Mir* could be resupplied. One man lived on *Mir* for 438 days.

2. Crossword Puzzle

Across

2. _____ was the United States's first space station.

4. The International Space Station orbits two _____ miles above the earth.

5. In 1986 _____ was launched.

Down

1. _____ was the Soviet Union's first space station.

2. The first country to send up a space station was the _____ _____.

3. _____ equipment was put on space stations to help people stay fit.

3. Number the events in the order that they happened.

A. ___ *Salyut 1* was launched.

B. ___ In 1986 the Soviet Union sent up another space station.

C. ___ *Skylab* was no longer used.

D. ___ A valve opened, and the crew died.

11

"A backyard carnival?" Jeff said to his brother, Colton, as they sat at their desks in their bedroom. "We can't have a backyard carnival."

"Yes we can," Colton said, holding up a basketball. "Look, we could toss basketballs into trash cans." He tossed the ball across the room. *Kerplunk.* It landed in the bottom of the garbage can. "We could do lots of things."

Jeff raised his eyebrows. "Maybe this isn't such a bad idea." His eyes widened. "And maybe we could make enough money to buy that video game at D-Mart."

Jeff and Colton spent the rest of the afternoon gathering what they needed for the carnival: basketballs for the ball toss, baseballs to throw at stacks of soda cans, empty pop bottles for a ring toss. Finally, they made a sign:

HAVE A FUN DAY AT OUR BACKYARD CARNIVAL,
THIS SATURDAY AT NOON.

The next day at school, Jeff and Colton's friends all said they would be coming to the carnival.

On Friday after school, Jeff and Colton set up the carnival. When they were finished, Jeff was excited. "We're going to make enough money to buy that video game."

Colton woke up Saturday morning to the sound of pounding rain. "Jeff! Look!"

Rain poured down. By noon, puddles nearly filled the backyard.

"I guess we'll have to cancel our carnival," Colton said.

"Yeah, now we won't be able to buy that video game," Jeff said.

Colton aimed a basketball at a trash can in their room. *Kerplunk.* Then he and Colton made another sign. They hung it on the tree over the old sign:

CARNIVAL CANCELLED,
BUT HAVE A FUN DAY ANYWAY!

1. Write *T* for true or *F* for false in the blank next to each sentence.
   A. ___ Jeff and Colton wanted to have a water fight.
   B. ___ Jeff and Colton wanted to earn money to buy a video game.
   C. ___ One of the carnival games was tossing a basketball into a dump truck.
   D. ___ When the carnival was cancelled, they told everyone to go jump in a lake.

2. Fill in the blank with the right word from the story.
   A. Jeff and Colton wanted to buy a video game at

   _____.

   B. Colton woke up Saturday morning to the sound of pounding _____.
   C. One of the games was throwing _____ at soda cans.
   D. Jeff and Colton wrote on their sign, "CARNIVAL CANCELLED, BUT HAVE A _____ DAY ANYWAY!

3. Match the sentence with the correct answer in the box.
   A. When Jeff and Colton talked about having their carnival, they were in their _____.
   B. Colton is Jeff's _____.
   C. Jeff and Colton set up the carnival on

   _____.

   D. The backyard was nearly filled with _____.

   > 1. rain puddles
   > 2. bedroom
   > 3. brother
   > 4. Friday

4. Bonus Word Play
   Synonyms are words that are spelled differently but have the same meaning. Find a synonym in the story for each of the following words:
   threw _____   horrible _____   ancient _____

What a Cricket Can Do

It's nighttime, and the air is hot. How hot? A thermometer can tell you how hot the air is, but so can the sound of a cricket chirping. That's right, cricket chirping is another way to tell what the temperature is.

To do this, you'll need to find a clock with a second hand. You'll also need to be able to hear a chirping cricket. Watch the second hand move forward for fifteen seconds. While you do that, count how many times a cricket chirps. Add forty to the number of cricket chirps you heard in fifteen seconds. The number you get will be about what the temperature is!

Crickets also do other interesting things. In some houses in Asia, crickets are household pets. There are two reasons why. First, the chirping sound of a cricket is thought to be very relaxing. Second, crickets can be good burglar alarms. Some people believe that once crickets know the sounds usually made around a home, they will stop chirping when a stranger is nearby.

Crickets chirp mostly at night. Only male crickets sing, or chirp. They chirp to catch the attention of a female cricket. They also chirp to scare off other males. Never keep more than one male cricket in a container because male crickets are so protective that they might kill each other.

A cricket's ears are located on the front of its legs. They look like tiny white spots and are barely visible to the human eye.

There's a famous story about a musical cricket named Chester. You may have read it. It's called *The Cricket in Times Square*.

14

1. Write *F* for fact or *O* for opinion in the blank next to each sentence.
   A. ___ Cricket chirping can be used to tell the temperature.
   B. ___ Using a cricket's chirp to tell the temperature is silly.
   C. ___ Crickets make cute household pets.
   D. ___ Crickets have ears on the front of their legs.

2. Fill in the blank with a word that makes sense in the sentence.
   A. A cricket's chirp and outdoor thermometers can both tell the _____.
   B. Crickets have legs; clocks have _____.
   C. Male crickets are very _____, so they should not be put in a jar together.
   D. Crickets' ears look like _____.

3. Circle the correct answer.
   A. Crickets are considered a household pet in _____.
      the zoo   a pet store   Asia

   B. To tell what the temperature is, a cricket's chirp should be counted for _____.
      5 seconds   15 minutes   15 seconds

   C. Male crickets also use chirping to scare off other _____.
      animals   males   females

   D. In Asia, crickets are sometimes used as _____.
      a burglar   a burglar alarm   a burglar's pet

15

Dear Mr. President,

My name is Kelsy Johnson, and I am in the fourth grade. I was just picked to be president of a club I have with my two best friends, Becky and Ann. The biggest job I have is making sure my room is clean before everyone comes over.

Now that I am a president, I was wondering some things. Would you please answer these questions for me?

- Are you ever afraid to be president?
- How early do you have to get up?
- What is your favorite breakfast cereal?
- Do you have to carry your own bowl to the sink when you are finished eating?
- Have you ever had a nightmare about being president?
- Do you ever get lonely?
- Do you receive a lot of presents for your birthday?
- Do you make a lot of money for being president?

I am glad to be the president of my club. I hope you are happy being president of the United States. If you ever need my help, just let me know. I think I know how to be a good president now.

Sincerely,

Kelsy

P.S. Please say hi to Mrs. President, and your dog too (someone told me you have a dog).

Reading Comprehension

1. Underline the cause, and circle the effect.
   A. I am the president of my club. I have to clean my room.
   B. I am wondering some things. Could you please answer my questions?
   C. If you need help, call me.
   D. Someone told me you have a dog. Please say hi to your dog.

2. Crossword Puzzle

   Across
   3. Kelsy is in the _____ grade.
   4. Kelsy asked the president if he had to take his own cereal bowl to the kitchen _____.
   6. Kelsy and her friends have a _____.

   Down
   1. Kelsy asked, "Are you ever _____ to be president?"
   2. Kelsy is the _____ of her club.
   5. the name of the girl who wrote the letter to the president

3. Number the sentences in the order that Kelsy wrote them.
   A. ___ I was wondering some things.
   B. ___ I know how to be a good president now.
   C. ___ I am in the fourth grade.
   D. ___ Someone told me you have a dog.

4. Bonus Word Play
   Homophones are words that have the same sound but are spelled differently. Find the right homophone for each word in the story.
   bee _____   no _____   high _____

Reading Grade 4—RBP0067

Hail

Flash! It's lightning. Crash! It's thunder. There is a pounding on the roof so loud that it can't be rain. What is it? It's hail.

Hail forms high above the earth in the thunderclouds. Hail usually falls right after or during a thunderstorm. The thunderclouds where hailstones are made are over 25,000 feet above the earth.

Hail is made of many layers of frozen rain. First, a raindrop forms at the bottom of a thundercloud where it is warm. Then the raindrop is blown to the top of the thundercloud where the air is moist and cold. The cold air freezes the raindrop. The frozen raindrop falls down to the bottom of the thundercloud where the warm air coats it again. This rain-coated hailstone bounces to the top of the cloud again, where it freezes once more. The hailstone continues to add water and then freeze until the hailstone is too heavy for the air to hold. Most hailstones are harmless, but some can cause a lot of damage.

Hailstones are usually the size of small peas. However, some hailstones can be the size of golf balls. Others have been known to be as big as softballs! Hail can break windshields, rip leaves off trees, or make dents in cars. Yet because it's ice, hail floats on water.

The largest hailstone on record fell in Kansas. It was more than five inches in diameter and weighed almost two pounds!

Reading Comprehension

1. Write *T* for true or *F* for false in the blank next to each sentence.

A. ___ Hail is made from big snowflakes.

B. ___ Hail floats.

C. ___ Hail falls from a thundercloud when it gets too heavy for the air to support it.

D. ___ Hail can break a horse's back.

2. Fill in the blank with the right word from the story.

A. Hail is made of many layers of frozen _____.

B. The first layer of rain falls down to the _____ of a thundercloud.

C. Hail makes _____ in cars.

D. Hail usually comes with a _____.

3. Match the sentence with the correct answer in the box.

A. Hailstones are made over _____ above the earth.

B. Once a raindrop is formed, it blows to the _____ of a thundercloud.

C. Some hailstones are the size of _____.

D. Hailstones can break a _____.

> 1. windshield
>
> 2. 25,000 feet
>
> 3. top
>
> 4. golf balls

4. Bonus Word Play

How many syllables are in each word?

lightning _____   usually _____   cause _____

©RBP Books

Ricky Goes to the Circus

Ricky was excited to go to the circus for his birthday with his friends, Mark and Bob. When they arrived, Ricky looked around. From their seats high in the stands, Ricky's father pointed out the huge ring on the ground in the middle of the huge tent.

"That must be where the ringmaster announces the show," Ricky said.

"And where all the animals do their tricks," Mark added.

Ropes were strung across the top of the tent. Big safety nets hung underneath them.

"That must be for the trapeze artists and the tightrope walkers," Mark said.

"I could never walk across something that high," Bob said.

"I could," said Ricky. Just then, music started playing, and the performers began to parade into the ring.

"I think the show is about to start," Ricky's father said.

Ricky and his friends watched elephants stand on their hind legs. Clowns juggled balls. Then, a lion tamer made two lions climb on chairs and sit. A lady stood on two horses as they galloped around the ring. At the end of the show, the ringmaster said, "Thank you for coming to the greatest show on earth."

Mark said, "That was the best."

"I think so too," said Bob.

"That's why it's the greatest show on earth," Ricky said.

1. Write *F* for fact or *O* for opinion in the blank next to each sentence.

A. ___ The circus takes place in a big tent.

B. ___ The lions looked mean.

C. ___ Trapeze artists swing on ropes hung high in the air.

D. ___ Music played in the background.

2. Write *S* for same or *D* for different in the blank next to each sentence.

A. ___ Ricky, Mark, and Bob all thought the circus was fun.

B. ___ Bob would never walk the tightrope, but Ricky said he would.

C. ___ Ricky looked up and saw a tightrope strung across the tent. His friends did, too.

D. ___ The elephants stood on their hind legs. The lions sat on chairs.

3. Circle the correct answer.

A. Ricky was excited to go to the circus for his _____.

    friend's birthday   father's birthday   birthday

B. The person who announces the show is called the _____.

    ringmaster   ringleader   bell ringer

C. The circus is the greatest _____ on earth.

    show   place   gift

D. A lady stood on two _____.

    tables   chairs   horses

4. Bonus Word Play

Unscramble the following word: N N N O E C U A S

_____

_____

Where the Sandwich Came From

In the early 1700s, a man named John Montagu was the Fourth Earl of Sandwich. An earl is like a duke or a baron. It is a position of wealth and importance.

John Montagu liked to play cards. In fact, he played cards all the time. Because he played so often, he often got hungry during a game. However, Montagu didn't know what to do about it. He could not eat a meal with both hands when one hand was holding cards.

One day he got hungry in the middle of a card game. The earl ordered his servants to put a slice of meat between two pieces of bread. He bit into this meal and liked it so much that he asked for it every time he played cards. Other people saw what Montagu was eating, and they thought his idea was a good one. When they got hungry, they asked for the same thing.

The sandwich became popular in the United States in the early 1800s. Americans learned how to make sandwiches when Elizabeth Leslie put the recipe in her cookbook. In the 1900s, sliced bread was invented. Since then, *sandwich* has become a household word.

Today billions of people eat sandwiches. They eat peanut butter and jelly sandwiches, tuna fish sandwiches, and egg salad sandwiches. There are pastrami sandwiches, club sandwiches, and finger sandwiches. But John Montagu, the Fourth Earl of Sandwich, will always be remembered for biting into that first handheld meal.

1. Underline the cause, and circle the effect.
   A. John Montagu could not eat with both hands. So he ordered a meal he could eat with one hand.
   B. Other people ordered sandwiches because they were hungry too.
   C. Elizabeth Leslie put the sandwich recipe in a cookbook. Americans learned how to make them.
   D. Sliced bread was invented. The sandwich became even more popular.

2. Crossword Puzzle

Across

2. Elizabeth Leslie put the _____ for a sandwich in a cookbook.
5. what John Montagu invented
6. John Montagu was the ____ Earl of Sandwich.

Down

1. When sliced _____ was invented, the sandwich became even more popular.
3. John Montagu loved playing _____.
4. the Fourth Earl of Sandwich's last name

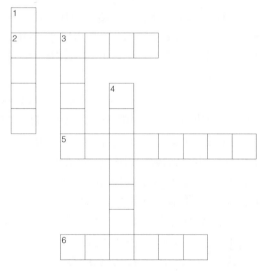

3. Number the events in the order that they happened.
   A. ___ Billions of people eat sandwiches.
   B. ___ One of Montagu's hands was always holding cards.
   C. ___ John Montagu liked playing cards.
   D. ___ Americans started eating sandwiches in the early 1800s.

The Talent Show

Mrs. Smith's fourth grade class was excited about the school talent show. Three students from the class were performing. Abby was going to play the piano. Morgan wanted to show everyone her new dance, and Tim was going to tell jokes.

The day of the talent show arrived. The principal, Miss Turnbow, surprised everyone by doing magic tricks. No one knew she was such a good magician. Miss Turnbow pulled a quarter out of someone's ear. She turned a chain of pretty scarves into colorful flowers, and then she pulled a real, live rabbit out of a hat.

When she was finished, the students clapped. Some of them even yelled, "Good job, Miss Turnbow, good job!"

The next person to perform was Abby. She played "Here Comes Santa Claus" on the piano. Everyone thought playing a Christmas song in the middle of May was strange, but they still clapped.

Morgan showed everyone her talent by doing a jazz dance. She made a few mistakes, but the students still liked it.

Then it was Tim's turn. Tim tried telling funny jokes, but no one laughed. He tried and tried, but his jokes weren't funny. Finally the time came for Tim to leave the stage. When he did, he tripped on the microphone cord. Everyone laughed so hard that Tim pretended to fall again. The students laughed even more. Tim decided that if he were ever in a talent show again, he wouldn't tell jokes. He would just pretend to trip a lot instead.

Reading Comprehension

1. Write *T* for true or *F* for false in the blank next to each sentence.
  A. ___ Morgan played a Christmas song on the piano.
  B. ___ Everyone laughed when Tim tripped.
  C. ___ Miss Turnbow turned pretty flowers into colorful scarves.
  D. ___ Mrs. Smith's class was upset about the talent show.

2. Fill in the blank with the right word from the story.
  A. Morgan performed a _____ dance.
  B. Everyone thought playing a Christmas song in the middle of _____ was strange.
  C. When Miss Turnbow finished her talent, some students yelled, "_____ _____."
  D. Mrs. Smith's _____ grade class was excited about the talent show.

3. Match the sentence with the correct answer in the box.
  A. When Abby was finished performing, the students _____.
  B. The students felt badly for _____.
  C. The students didn't laugh at Tim's _____.
  D. Miss Turnbow pulled a quarter out of someone's _____.

  1. tripped
  2. ear
  3. talent
  4. clapped

4. Bonus Word Play

talent   pretty
microphone funny
rabbit   stage
magician   tripped

```
m p t r i p p e d n
v i b s t a g e a m
y y c c d z k i t a
k t y r m o c t n n
s w t g o i f v e m
a n v e g p c q l v
v n f a r l h m a q
k c m g r p k o t b
r t i b b a r x n c
k s d y n n u f s e
```

25

The woods are full of fairies!
The trees are all alive;
The river overflows with them,
See how they dip and dive!
What funny little fellows!
What dainty little dears!
They dance and leap, and prance and peep,
And utter fairy cheers!

I'd like to tame a fairy,
To keep it on a shelf,
To see it wash its little face,
And dress its little self.
I'd teach it pretty manners,
It always should say, "Please!"
And then, you know, I'd make it sew,
And curtsy with its knees!

Reading Comprehension

1. Pretend the poem is true. Write *F* for fact or *O* for opinion in the blank next to each sentence.
   A. ___ The woods are full of fairies!
   B. ___ What funny little fellows!
   C. ___ The trees are all alive!
   D. ___ They dance and leap, and prance and peep.

2. Write *S* for same or *D* for different in the blank next to each sentence.
   A. ___ prance and leap
   B. ___ trees and leaves
   C. ___ dainty and funny
   D. ___ little and small

3. Circle the correct answer.
   A. The river overflows with _____.

   fairies   fish   food

   B. The fairies utter fairy _____.

   cries   cheers   songs

   C. The child in the poem would like to _____ a fairy.

   buy   tame   sell

   D. The child in the story would also like to make the fairy

   _____.

   work   laugh   sew

4. Bonus Word Play
   Synonyms are words that are spelled differently but have the same meaning. Find the synonym in the poem for each of the following words:
   shouts _____
   instruct _____
   beautiful _____

Reading Grade 4—RBP0067

Wolfgang Amadeus Mozart

Wolfgang Amadeus Mozart was a great *composer*. A composer is someone who writes music. Mozart started playing the *harpsichord* when he was three years old. The harpsichord is like a piano. Mozart started to compose music when he was only five years old. When Mozart was six, he gave concerts. If the people didn't listen, he would stop playing and start to cry.

Mozart was born in Austria in 1756. His father wrote music and played the violin. He taught Mozart almost everything he knew about music, including how to play the violin. Everyone liked Mozart. He was a happy boy with a lot of talent.

When Mozart was fourteen, he became a *concertmaster*. A concertmaster is the person who leads the violin section in an orchestra. A concertmaster is also an assistant to the conductor. The *conductor* is the person who leads the entire orchestra.

Mozart continued to write music, teach, and perform, but he didn't make very much money. He ended up very poor.

One day a stranger asked Mozart to write a *requiem*. A requiem is a type of music played for a funeral. Mozart was not feeling well at the time, but he began writing the requiem. Some say he may have been thinking about his own life at the time.

Mozart worked so hard on this piece of music that he grew weaker and weaker. He became very ill, and he died before the requiem was finished. Because he had no money, Mozart was buried in an unmarked, poor person's grave. However, today Mozart is remembered as one of the most famous composers in the world.

28

1. Underline the cause, and circle the effect.
   A. When people didn't listen to him play the piano, Mozart started to cry.
   B. His father played the violin. He taught Mozart how to play it too.
   C. Mozart became a concertmaster. He wasn't paid well.
   D. Mozart was a happy boy. People liked him.

2. Crossword Puzzle

Across
3. Wolfgang Amadeus _____
5. a type of music played at a funeral
6. how old Mozart was when he started writing music

Down
1. a person who writes music
2. the person who taught Mozart almost everything he knew about music
4. where Mozart was born

3. Number the events in the order that they happened.
   A. ___ Mozart became very weak.
   B. ___ His father taught him everything he knew about music.
   C. ___ If the people wouldn't listen, Mozart would start to cry.
   D. ___ Mozart became a concertmaster.

The Wonderful Life of Dr. Seuss

Dr. Seuss wrote many books. His most famous book was *The Cat in the Hat*. He wrote it in 1957. He also wrote *Green Eggs and Ham* and *The Grinch Who Stole Christmas*.

Dr. Seuss was born in Springfield, Massachusetts, in 1904. He was given the name Theodor Seuss Geisel when he was born, but he used the name Dr. Seuss as his *pen name*. A pen name is a name a person uses when he or she writes a book. Dr. Seuss's pen name came from his middle name, which was also his mother's maiden name.

Dr. Seuss's mother loved reading books to her children. Every night before they went to bed, his mother would read them stories. She especially liked reading books that rhymed. Dr. Seuss said his mother was one of the reasons he wrote the kind of books he did.

The first book Dr. Seuss wrote was *And to Think That I Saw It on Mulberry Street*. He wrote this book in 1937. He wrote his last book in 1990. It was titled *Oh, the Places You'll Go*.

Dr. Seuss wrote forty-six children's books in all. His books have been translated into twenty different languages, including braille, so the blind can read them too. In all, Dr. Seuss's books have sold more than 200 million copies.

Some people believe Dr. Seuss even invented the word *nerd*. It appeared in a book that he wrote in 1950 titled *If I Ran the Zoo*.

Reading Comprehension

1. Write *T* for true or *F* for false in the blank next to each sentence.
   A. ___ Dr. Seuss's pen name came from his father.
   B. ___ Every night before they went to bed, his mother read her children stories.
   C. ___ The word *nerd* might have been created by Dr. Seuss.
   D. ___ *And to Think That I Saw It on Mulberry Street* was written in 1960.

2. Fill in the blank with the right word from the story.
   A. The name _____ _____ _____ was given to Dr. Seuss when he was born.
   B. Dr. Seuss was born in Springfield, _____.
   C. When an author doesn't use his or her real name, he or she uses a _____ name.
   D. The most famous book written by Dr. Seuss was

   _____.

3. Match the sentence with the correct answer in the box.
   A. In 1957 Dr. Seuss wrote _____.
   B. The word *nerd* came from the book _____.
   C. The last book Dr. Seuss wrote was _____.
   D. The first book written by Dr. Seuss was _____.

   ┌─────────────────────────────────┐
   │ 1. *Oh, the Places You'll Go*   │
   │ 2. *The Cat in the Hat*   │
   │ 3. *If I Ran the Zoo*   │
   │ 4. *And to Think That I Saw*   │
   │   *It on Mulberry Street*   │
   └─────────────────────────────────┘

4. Bonus Word Play
   Homophones are words that have the same sound but are spelled differently. Find the right homophone in the story for each word.
   won _____
   right_____
   knight _____

"I can't do this!" Megan said to her best friend, Kim. The roller coaster raced past again. People screamed. Megan's heart pounded, and her throat felt dry. She swallowed hard.

Kim smiled as they stood in line. "Yes, you can. It's easy."

"It's too high and too fast," Megan said as people moved forward, taking Kim and Megan closer to the front of the line.

"Just pretend you're sitting on a chair, watching television," Kim said.

"I wish I was," Megan moaned.

"You'll be okay," Kim said. "I ride this all the time."

The roller coaster stopped in front of them. People got off; then more got on. Ten people now stood between Megan and the roller coaster. What was she going to do? She looked around. Maybe she could tell Kim she felt sick or had a bad heart. People who were sick or had bad hearts weren't supposed to ride the roller coaster.

Megan closed her eyes and took a deep breath. Maybe she could close her eyes and count to one hundred during the ride. The ride would certainly be over by then. The roller coaster stopped in front of them. It looked like a big, mean, mechanical dragon.

"Step into the car," the attendant said.

Megan and Kim climbed into the seat. They pulled the safety bar closed. The ride began. It climbed slowly up the hill, then raced down. Kim put her hands up in the air while Megan closed her eyes. Megan counted to one hundred, but the ride was still going. By the time she reached 117, the ride was over. She opened one eye and saw Kim looking at her.

"There, aren't roller coasters fun?" Kim asked.

Reading Comprehension

1. Write *F* for fact or *O* for opinion in the blank next to each sentence.

A. ___ Kim was Megan's best friend.

B. ___ Roller coasters are a lot of fun.

C. ___ The roller coaster looked like a mean, mechanical dragon.

D. ___ Amusement parks should make roller coaster rides faster.

2. Circle the correct answer.

A. Kim told Megan she should pretend like she was sitting on a _____.

couch   toadstool   chair

B. Because Megan did not want to ride the roller coaster, she thought she might tell Kim she was _____.

crazy   too young   sick

C. Megan and Kim climbed into their seats and pulled the _____ closed.

teeth   shoes   safety bar

D. Megan _____ the whole way.

laughed   counted   screamed

3. Answer the following questions about the story.

A. The people on the roller coaster all _____.

B. How are Megan and Kim different?

_____

C. What did Megan think the roller coaster looked like?

_____

D. How was the ride up the hill different from the ride down the hill?

_____

The Unbelievable World of Crocodiles

Crocodiles eat rocks. It's true. Crocodiles eat rocks to help them digest their food. And they don't just eat a few rocks. They eat 10 to 15 pounds of them! Rocks not only help with a crocodile's digestion, they also help a crocodile stay underwater longer. Sometimes a crocodile will stay underwater for as long as one hour.

Crocodiles may eat rocks, but they don't actually eat food very often. In fact, they only get hungry about once a week.

Even though their brains are only the size of a small banana, crocodiles are the most intelligent of all reptiles. Crocodiles are also the largest reptiles.

Crocodiles may even have something in common with dogs. Some people believe a crocodile will hold its mouth open to cool off, like when a dog pants because it's too hot.

A crocodile can grow to be 27 feet long. This is about the size of three medium-sized cars lined up end to end. Mother crocodiles lay eggs. Once their babies hatch, they carry them around in their mouths. This keeps the babies safe.

Crocodiles learn by watching what other animals do. If an animal comes to the water at the same time each day, a crocodile will learn that this is the best time to catch it.

To help them see and swim at the same time, crocodiles have a third eyelid. This eyelid works a lot like swimming goggles. But I wouldn't ask a crocodile to show you how it works if I were you!

1. Underline the cause, and circle the effect.
   A. Crocodiles eat rocks. Rocks help them stay underwater.
   B. To help it stay cool, a crocodile opens its mouth.
   C. Mother crocodiles need to protect their young. They carry their babies in their mouths.
   D. Crocodiles watch other animals. Then they know when to catch them.

2. Crossword Puzzle

   Across
   1. Crocodiles eat these.
   3. Rocks help a crocodile's

      _____.
   5. Crocodiles have three of these.

   Down
   2. a large, lizard-like creature
   4. a cold-blooded creature
   6. A crocodile is the _____ reptile.

3. Number the events in the order that they are told about in the story.
   A. ___ Mother crocodiles lay eggs.
   B. ___ Their eyelids work like swimming goggles.
   C. ___ Crocodiles can grow up to 27 feet long.
   D. ___ They can stay underwater for up to an hour.

4. Bonus Word Play
   Unscramble the following word: N   T   F   F   E   E   I

The Treasure Hunt

"What is it?" Casey asked Shawn as they looked at the paper Shawn held in his hands.

"It's a clue," Shawn said. "Billy's mom said each clue is a rhyming riddle. When we figure out all the clues, we'll know where the treasure is."

Shawn looked at the other kids at Billy's birthday party. They were reading their clues also.

"I wonder what's in the treasure chest." Daniel imagined it filled with money. "This is going to be fun."

Shawn read the riddle out loud. "Roses are red, violets are blue. If you wrote a letter, putting it here is what you would do."

"The mailbox!" Casey shouted.

Shawn and Casey ran to the mailbox. Other boys followed.

Casey read the next clue to Shawn. "Mary had a little lamb; its fleece was white as snow. But if Mary had this clue to read, underneath the trash is where she'd go."

Casey hollered, "The trash cans!"

Casey and Shawn ran to the trash can and pulled the next clue out from underneath it. They went from clue to clue. Finally they found the last one inside the gas barbecue grill. "Now that this hunt is over, you'll find the treasure chest next to our dog, Rover." Casey and Shawn ran to Rover. Next to him was a treasure chest. They opened it. It was filled with candy.

"That was fun," Shawn said, unwrapping a piece of candy.

"This is the best part," Casey said, filling his pockets.

1. Write *T* for true or *F* for false in the blank next to each sentence.
   A. ___ Casey and Shawn were at a Christmas party.
   B. ___ The last clue they found was in the barbecue grill.
   C. ___ Inside the treasure chest was lots of money.
   D. ___ Each clue used a rhyming riddle.

2. Fill in the blank with the right word from the story.
   A. The treasure chest was next to _____.
   B. Casey and Shawn were at a _____ _____.
   C. _____ figured out the first clue.
   D. One of the clues said, "_____ had a little lamb."

3. Match the sentence with the correct answer in the box.
   A. Casey and Shawn had to figure out

   _____.
   B. The clues led them to _____.
   C. The treasure chest was next to _____.
   D. Rover was Billy's _____.

   1. dog
   2. each clue
   3. the treasure
   4. Rover

4. Bonus Word Play
   Antonyms are words that have opposite meanings. Find the antonym in the story for each of the following words:
   closed _____
   empty _____
   above _____

Static Electricity

A boy walks across the carpet. He touches a doorknob, and zap! A girl combs her hair on a cold, winter morning. Her hair sticks up all over. What makes this happen? Static electricity.

Static electricity is easy to understand once you learn about atoms.

Atoms are the tiny building blocks that make up everything. Atoms are filled with protons, neutrons, and electrons. Protons have a positive charge of energy. Electrons have a negative charge. Positive and negative charges attract one another. When they bump into each other, they stick.

Positive charges don't attract other positive charges. Negative charges don't attract other negative charges either. So when two positives or two negatives bump each other, they don't stick. They push each other away.

When you walk across a carpet, your shoes pick up electrons from the carpet. This negative energy flies around you, looking for positive energy to attach to. A doorknob has positive energy, or protons. So the negative energy from your body leaps toward the positive energy of the doorknob. Zap! You get static electricity.

Lightning is like static electricity too—only bigger!

1. Write *F* for fact or *O* for opinion in the blank next to each sentence.

A. ___ The world should get rid of static electricity.

B. ___ An atom is a tiny thing.

C. ___ Lightning is like static electricity, only bigger.

D. ___ Negative energy should be stopped.

2. Write *S* for same or *D* for different in the blank next to each sentence.

A. ___ Shoes and combs pick up negative energy.

B. ___ Protons have positive energy. Electrons have negative energy.

C. ___ Lightning has protons and electrons. So does static electricity.

D. ___ Protons and electrons move away from each other.

3. Circle the correct answer.

A. A boy walks across carpet, touches a doorknob, and _____.

    whoops   zap   hello

B. An atom is filled with _____.

    static   electricity   neutrons

C. When energies have different charges, they will _____.

    fight   go out to lunch   attract each other

D. A doorknob has _____.

    germs   positive energy   negative energy

4. Bonus Word Play—Word Search

static	positive
proton	negative
neutron	atom
electron	energy

```
g  e  n  a  r  y  e  l
n  l  e  v  e  g  v  b
o  e  g  n  c  r  i  d
r  c  a  o  i  e  t  t
t  t  t  t  t  n  i  a
u  r  i  o  a  e  s  t
e  o  v  r  t  b  o  o
n  n  e  p  s  o  p  m
```

Louisa May Alcott

Louisa May Alcott was born in Germantown, Pennsylvania, but she lived most of her life in Massachusetts. Her father was a smart man who taught her many things. The famous writers Ralph Waldo Emerson and Henry David Thoreau were close family friends. Louisa loved to write too. She grew up with people who loved writing. They helped her become a famous author.

When Louisa was sixteen years old, her family needed money. Louisa wanted to help. She went to work as a servant, seamstress, teacher, and governess. During this time, she started writing poems and short stories. Her first collection of short stories was called *Flower Fables*. She wrote them in 1854 to entertain Ralph Waldo Emerson's daughter.

Her most popular book was *Little Women*. This book was published in 1868. *Little Women* is the story of a family who lived during the Civil War. This family was really Louisa's family. In the book, Louisa was one of the main characters. Her name in the book was Jo.

Louisa never married. She passed away in 1888, two days after her father died. In 1996, nearly one hundred years after Louisa died, another book she had written was found. She wrote it in 1849 when she was 18. It is called *The Inheritance*. It is the first book written by Louisa May Alcott.

www.summerbridgeactivities.com   © RBP Books

Reading Comprehension

1. Underline the cause, and circle the effect.

   A. Louisa loved writing. She became famous.

   B. Louisa went to work. She became a seamstress.

   C. *The Inheritance* was found after Louisa died. It was published.

   D. She wrote *Flower Fables*. She wanted to entertain Emerson's daughter.

2. Crossword Puzzle

Across

2. Louisa's last name

5. one of the jobs Alcott took to help her family with their money problems

Down

1. Her most famous book was _____ *Women.*

3. _____ May Alcott

4. A person who writes books is called an author or a _____.

6. One book was about a family who lived during the _____ War.

3. Number the events in the order that they were told.

   A. ___ Louisa was one of the main characters in her book *Little Women*.

   B. ___ Emerson and Thoreau were close family friends.

   C. ___ Louisa worked as a seamstress.

   D. ___ Louisa grew up with people who loved writing.

Firefly Facts

Fireflies look like tiny, twinkling stars. But really they are tiny, flying creatures. Fireflies have two chemicals in them that give off light when they are mixed together. The light is either green or yellow and comes from under a firefly's belly. The light from some fireflies flickers on and off. Other fireflies give off light that glows constantly. Fireflies aren't the only things that light up. Their eggs do too.

When fireflies become upset, their light glows brighter. This reminds their enemies that the chemicals that make them light up also taste and smell bad.

Because they are called fireflies, most people think fireflies are flies. But they are really beetles. Fireflies are also called lightning bugs. Fireflies without wings are called glowworms. Most glowworms live in Europe. In Asia there are fireflies that live underwater.

In America fireflies live only in the eastern United States. No one knows why fireflies do not live in the western United States.

All winged insects have two sets of wings, except fireflies. They have only one set of wings. Fireflies fly only at night. In the daytime, they hide. Fireflies love to live in rotting wood, in forested areas, and by streams or ponds.

Fireflies are one of the few bugs that are not eaten by other creatures. That's good news if you're a firefly, or if you just like to watch them.

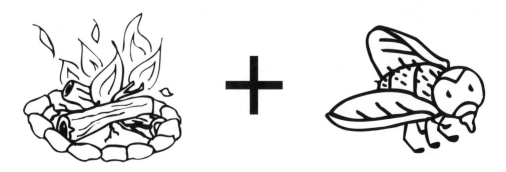

1. Write *T* for true or *F* for false in the blank next to each sentence.
   A. ___ Fireflies live only in the western part of the United States.
   B. ___ Fireflies smell nice.
   C. ___ Fireflies are flies.
   D. ___ A firefly without wings is called a beetle.

2. Fill in the blank with the right word from the story.
   A. Fireflies only fly at night because they _____ in the daytime.
   B. A firefly's light comes from two _____ mixing together.
   C. Most _____ live in Europe.
   D. Fireflies have only _____ set of wings.

3. Match the sentence with the correct answer in the box.
   A. In Asia some fireflies live

      _____.

   B. Another name for *firefly* is

      _____.

   C. Fireflies like to live _____.
   D. No fireflies live in the _____ United States.

   > 1. lightning bug
   > 2. near streams or ponds
   > 3. underwater
   > 4. western

4. Bonus Word Play
   Homographs are words that are spelled the same but have different meanings. Circle the definition for the correct homograph used in the story.
   A. fly   a flying insect   bait used fishing
   B. star   shines at night   famous person
   C. bug   an insect   bother

Dear Diary,

Today was a crazy day. First, the bathroom flooded, so when I woke up, water was dripping through my ceiling. Then we were out of milk, so I didn't have any for my cereal. Then, when I got to school, I remembered I forgot my homework. Plus, now I've got the chicken pox, and no one else in my class has them! Things could be worse, though. My best friend, Sarah, broke her leg yesterday riding her bike. I'm glad that didn't happen to me.

I like having a diary. It gives me someone to talk to. It's like having me as my own best friend. Sarah has a diary too. I just hope my little brother, Billy, doesn't find this book. He'd tell everybody all my secrets, like how I like Mark. Then Mark would find out. He would tell everyone, and I would be so embarrassed.

Anyway, now that I've got the chicken pox, I'm not going to be able to go to school. I always thought that would be fun, but I'm already bored, and I haven't even missed school yet. I itch like crazy. I hope this goes away soon.

Tonight Mom said she would fix me my favorite meal, macaroni and cheese. Billy hates macaroni and cheese. Dad said he would bring home some movies to watch. Maybe that will help.

Oh well, I guess I should go now. Not that I have anything important to do. It's just that my hand is getting tired.

Talk to you tomorrow,

Carmen

Reading Comprehension

1. Write *F* for fact or *O* for opinion in the blank next to each sentence.
   A. ___ The bathroom flooded.
   B. ___ Breaking a leg hurts.
   C. ___ Keeping a diary is good for people.
   D. ___ Staying home from school would be fun.

2. Answer the following questions about the story.
   A. What is a physical difference between Carmen and Sarah?

   _____

   B. How are Carmen and Sarah the same? _____

   _____

   C. Name one thing that makes Carmen and Billy different.

   _____

   D. What is the difference between Carmen and the rest of the class? _____

   _____

3. Circle the correct answer.
   A. Carmen quit writing because _____.
      her hand was getting tired

      her chicken pox itched

      Sarah was coming over
   B. When Carmen got to school, she realized she had forgotten her _____.
      homework   lunch   diary
   C. If Billy read her diary, Carmen was afraid he would tell all her _____.
      secrets   problems   jokes
   D. Carmen hadn't missed school yet, but she was already _____.
      happy   sad   bored

The first fire truck was invented in the 1720s. It was called the Little Newshan. Before then, people formed *bucket brigades*. A church bell might ring to let townspeople know there was a fire. People would run to the burning building and make a line that stretched from the fire to the closest place they could get water. Standing side-by-side, they passed buckets of water from one person to the next. The last person in line would throw the water on the fire.

In the early 1800s, horses pulled fire trucks. The horses wore special shirts to keep them from being hurt by the flames. The shirts also helped people see the horses. Sometimes firefighters pulled the fire trucks themselves.

The first fire trucks had hand pumps. Firefighters pumped water from a reservoir on the truck. The Little Newshan could spray about sixty gallons of water a minute. That's about twice as much as a garden hose. Steam-powered fire trucks were made in 1852. Motorized fire trucks were invented in the early 1900s. Before fire trucks had sirens, firefighters used bells and whistles to let people know they were coming. Sometimes firefighting companies would race to be the first on the scene so they could use the public hydrants. Some companies even had men watch the fireplug until the fire truck could get there.

Benjamin Franklin formed the first volunteer fire department in the 1700s. Some towns still have volunteer fire departments today.

Reading Comprehension

1. Underline the cause, and circle the effect.
   A. The Little Newshan was built. People didn't carry buckets of water to a fire.
   B. If people passed buckets of water to the fire, the fire could be put out.
   C. So the horses would not get hurt, they wore special shirts.
   D. Sirens were put on fire trucks. Bells were no longer used.

2. Crossword Puzzle

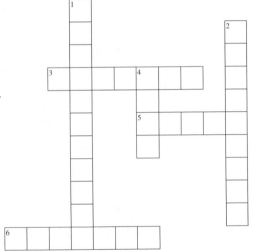

   Across
   3. the first fire truck: Little _____
   5. lets people know a fire truck is coming
   6. Firefighters raced each other to the scene so they could use this.

   Down
   1. a person who fights a fire
   2. a firefighter who didn't get paid
   4. Water sprays out of this.

3. Number the events in the order that they were told.
   A. ___ Horses pulled fire trucks.
   B. ___ A church bell would warn people of a fire.
   C. ___ Firefighters used bells and whistles.
   D. ___ Each horse wore a special shirt.

4. Bonus Word Play
   How many syllables are in each word?
   reservoir _____
   companies _____
   would _____

47

Aesop

Aesop (pronounced ee-sop) was a famous storyteller. He was born in Greece about 620 B.C. Not a lot is known about Aesop. Some people say he was an ugly man who was very smart. Aesop liked telling stories that shared lessons about life. His stories used animals instead of people. This kind of tale is called a fable.

Aesop was born a slave. Two masters owned him. His second master let Aesop go because he thought Aesop was so smart. Aesop became well known for his stories. His stories were passed from person to person. They were not written down until 200 years after his death.

Because he liked to travel, Aesop lived in a lot of different places. For a while he lived in Sardis. Sardis was the capital city of Lydia, which was ruled by a famous king. This king liked learning and had a lot of friends. Aesop ended up working for the king. During this time, Aesop was given money to give to the people of Delphi. Aesop felt the people were not honest, so he refused to give them the money. Because of this, the people of Delphi pushed him over a cliff to his death.

During his lifetime, Aesop created 655 fables. Many of these fables are still well known today. One of his most famous tales is "The Tortoise and the Hare."

1. Write *T* for true or *F* for false in the blank next to each sentence.
   A. ___ Aesop was a king.
   B. ___ A fable is a story about life using animals instead of people.
   C. ___ Aesop refused to give the people their money.
   D. ___ Aesop was a nice looking man who wasn't very smart.

2. Fill in the blank with the right word from the story.
   A. Aesop traveled to a lot of different places, including

   _____.

   B. His second master let Aesop go because he thought Aesop was _____.
   C. Aesop's stories were not written down until _____ years after his death.
   D. Aesop was born in _____ in the year_____.

3. Match the sentence with the correct answer in the box.
   A. One of the places Aesop lived was _____.
   B. Aesop liked telling stories about life _____.
   C. The people pushed Aesop over a _____.
   D. Aesop felt the people were not _____.

   | 1. cliff |
   | 2. honest |
   | 3. Sardis |
   | 4. lessons |

4. Bonus Word Play
   Unscramble the following word: S O A P E

   _____

   _____

Aesop's Fable: The Tortoise and the Hare

Once upon a time, there was a tortoise that moved very slowly. One day, while traveling through the forest, the tortoise met a hare. When the hare saw how slowly the tortoise moved, the hare made fun of him. The tortoise was not bothered by the hare's teasing. Instead, the tortoise challenged the hare to a race.

"Because you run so fast, you have to keep stopping. One of these days you will stop and be too tired to start again," said the tortoise.

The hare laughed. "You're wrong. You are so slow, you'll never cross the finish line."

When the day of the race arrived, all the animals in the forest gathered to watch.

Some said, "If the race is a long one, I think the hare will lose because he always runs so fast, he will run out of energy."

"I think the tortoise will lose," said others. "He is so slow that he will never finish the race."

The tortoise and the hare stood on the starting line. The race began. The hare ran off, leaving the tortoise behind.

Soon the hare began to tire. "I'm far ahead of the tortoise," he said. "I have plenty of time to get to the finish line. I'll lie down here and take a little nap."

So the hare slept while the tortoise plodded slowly along at a steady pace.

When the animals saw the tortoise as he got near the finish line, they started cheering for him. The cheering woke up the hare. The hare saw the tortoise near the end of the race and began running, but it was too late. The tortoise had won the race.

Reading Comprehension

1. Write *F* for fact or *O* for opinion in the blank next to each sentence.
   A. ___ A hare could never lose a race.
   B. ___ The tortoise was slow.
   C. ___ A tortoise could never win a race.
   D. ___ The hare was fast.

2. Write *S* for same or *D* for different in the blank next to each sentence.
   A. ___ All of the animals watched the race.
   B. ___ The hare was fast. The tortoise was slow.
   C. ___ Some of the animals thought the hare would win the race; others thought the tortoise would.
   D. ___ The tortoise and the hare were both traveling through the forest.

3. Circle the correct answer.
   A. The hare ran so fast that he got tired and _____.
      cried   fell asleep   lied

   B. The tortoise was slow, but he _____.
      kept going   was cute   sang

   C. The tortoise and the hare began the race at the
      _____.
      store   pond   starting line

   D. The tortoise won the _____.
      prize   race   money

4. Bonus Word Play
   Antonyms are words that have opposite meanings. Find the antonym in the story for each of the following words:
   fast _____
   never _____
   right_____

Who Lost Their Black Dog?

Annie was sitting in the front seat of the car while her mother drove. As she looked out the window, she saw a sign on a telephone pole. The sign read:

Lost, small, black dog with fluffy ears.

Family misses her.

Dog's name is Lady.

If found, call 213-0005.

Annie remembered when her family had lost their dog, Buster. Annie had missed him so much that she couldn't sleep until Buster had been found. She wondered if this family had a little girl who missed Lady. She decided that she wanted to help this family find their dog.

The next day at school, Annie asked her friends if any of them had seen a small, black dog with fluffy ears. Everyone said no, except for one classmate.

"I saw a dog like that in my neighbor's backyard," Tom said. "And they've never had a dog before." Annie could hardly believe it. Maybe she had found the lost dog. After school, she went with Tom to talk to his neighbor.

"Did the dog have fluffy ears?" she asked Tom while they walked.

"I don't know," Tom said. Annie hoped it did.

At the neighbor's house, Tom knocked on the door. A tiny old woman answered.

"I was wondering if you've seen a small, black dog with fluffy ears?" Annie said.

The lady smiled. "Yes, I have. It is in my backyard. I was keeping it there so it wouldn't get run over."

Annie was excited. She gave Tom's neighbor the phone number she had seen on the sign. While Tom's neighbor went inside to call, Tom and Annie went to the gate and called for Lady. The dog picked up its ears and trotted over.

"It's got to be her," Annie said.

Reading Comprehension

1. Underline the cause, and circle the effect.
   A. Annie looked out the car window. She saw a sign on a telephone pole.
   B. Everyone said no when Annie asked if anyone had seen a small, black dog.
   C. Annie's family missed their dog when they lost her.
   D. Tom knocked on the door. A tiny, old lady answered.

2. Crossword Puzzle

   Across
   2. The sign said, "_____, small, black dog."
   3. Annie saw this on the telephone pole.
   4. What did the family lose?
   5. The lost dog had _____ ears.

   Down
   1. Annie and Tom _____ the dog.
   3. Annie asked everyone at _____ if they had seen the lost dog.

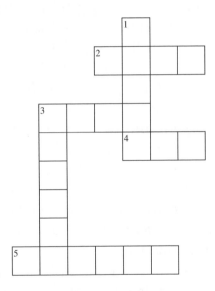

3. Number the events in the order that they happened.
   A. ___ Annie gave Tom's neighbor the phone number she saw on the sign.
   B. ___ Annie sat in the front seat of the car.
   C. ___ Tom said he had seen a dog.
   D. ___ A tiny, old woman answered the door.

Where Bubble Gum Came From

The first bubble gum salesmen went from store to store blowing big bubbles. They hoped store owners would buy the gum once they saw what it could do.

Walter Diemer taught the salesmen how to blow bubbles. Why Walter Diemer? Because Walter Diemer invented bubble gum.

Walter Diemer was 23 years old when he invented bubble gum. Diemer was an accountant for a gum company called Fleer. When he wasn't keeping track of money, he experimented with gum. One of his experiments resulted in something different. It was gum that was chewy but not as sticky as regular gum. It was perfect for blowing bubbles.

Bubble gum is made from a gum base. The first gum base was made from *chicle*. Chicle is a rubbery sap from the bark of a tree found in Central America. Today gum base is made from pine tree rosin. Or it can be a man-made ingredient made from petroleum. The gum base is mixed with sugar, artificial coloring, artificial flavors, and other ingredients.

To blow a good bubble, chew the bubble gum until it is soft or until it no longer tastes sweet. Flatten the gum between your tongue and front teeth. Then use your tongue to push the gum out of your mouth. Blow slowly until the bubble forms.

Unfortunately, sugar-free gum is not good for making big bubbles.

www.summerbridgeactivities.com

Reading Comprehension

1. Write *T* for true or *F* for false in the blank next to each sentence.
   A. ___ The first gum base was made from the fruit of a tree.
   B. ___ Today gum base is made from pine tree rosin.
   C. ___ Walter Diemer taught salesmen to blow bubbles.
   D. ___ Sugar-free gum is good for blowing bubbles.

2. Fill in the blank with the right word from the story.
   A. _____ were the first people who blew bubbles.
   B. Walter Diemer was _____ years old when he invented bubble gum.
   C. Diemer worked for a company called _____.
   D. The gum base is mixed with _____ flavoring.

3. Match the sentence with the correct answer in the box.
   A. To blow a good bubble, chew on the gum until it is _____.
   B. At the Fleer company, Walter Diemer was in charge of the _____.
   C. The first gum was made from _____.
   D. Gum is made from a man-made ingredient called _____.

   > 1. chicle
   > 2. petroleum
   > 3. money
   > 4. soft

4. Bonus Word Play
   Synonyms are words that have the same or almost the same meaning. Find the synonym in the story for each of the following words:
   gooey_____
   wished_____
   created _____

Breakfast in Bed

Daniel sat up in bed and looked over at his brother, Austin. "Let's fix Mom breakfast in bed."

Austin rubbed his eyes, trying to wake up. "Why?"

"Because it would be fun."

Austin shrugged his shoulders. "Okay."

Still in their pajamas, Daniel and Austin ran down to the kitchen. Daniel opened the refrigerator and looked inside. "We don't have any eggs."

Austin opened the cupboard. "We don't have any bread either." He closed the cupboard door. "What are we going to do?"

Daniel moved some containers in the refrigerator. He pulled out a blue bowl. "We've got pudding. Pudding has eggs in it."

Austin looked in the cupboard. He showed Daniel a box. "We have crackers. Crackers are like toast."

Daniel got a plate and set it on the counter on top of a small piece of yellow paper. He put some pudding on the plate. Austin added the crackers.

"Mom's going to love this," Austin said.

Daniel and Austin went to their mother's room, but she wasn't there. They looked all over the house but couldn't find her. They found their older sister, Kelly, asleep in bed, but their mother was nowhere around.

Daniel and Austin went back into the kitchen. Daniel set the plate on the counter. When he did, he noticed a yellow piece of paper with a note written on it. The note said, "Went to the dentist. Be back soon. Mom."

"What are we going to do?" Austin asked Daniel.

Daniel and Austin looked at the plate of food. Then they turned on the television and sat on the couch to eat their mother's breakfast.

Reading Comprehension

1. Write *F* for fact or *O* for opinion in the blank next to each sentence.
   A. ___ Daniel sat up in bed.
   B. ___ Making breakfast for their mom was a great idea.
   C. ___ I hope they cleaned up.
   D. ___ Austin added the crackers.

2. Fill in the blanks with the word that makes the most sense.
   A. The boys used pudding as a substitute for _____.
   B. They used crackers as a substitute for_____.
   C. When they decided to make their mother breakfast in bed, Daniel and Austin were both in their _____.
   D. Daniel and Austin are_____.

3. Circle the correct answer.
   A. Austin opened the _____.
      refrigerator   window   cupboard

   B. Daniel set the plate on _____.
      his lap   the table   a yellow paper

   C. Daniel and Austin's mother was _____.
      asleep   talking on the phone   gone

   D. Daniel and Austin turned on the television and then
      _____.
      played games   did dishes   ate their mother's breakfast

How Movies Got Their Start

A movie is made from a series of photographs. These photographs are put together in a row. The row of pictures moves so quickly that people see one smooth picture. Twenty-four pictures make up one second of a movie.

Thomas Edison helped invent movies when he made the *kinetoscope*. The kinetoscope is a box with a small hole in it. When people looked in it, they saw a five-second movie. People loved these little movies.

A man named Laurie Dickson worked for Thomas Edison. Dickson also liked the idea of moving pictures. He made a camera and filmed his first movie. It was called *Monkey Shines*.

Dickson wanted to make a movie projector to show the movie on a wall or screen. That way a lot of people could watch it at the same time. Edison didn't like this idea, so Dickson made the first movie projector while Edison was on vacation. Eventually, Dickson and Edison stopped working together.

Edison set up the first movie studio in 1893. That same year, Edison's assistant, Fred Ott, sneezed in front of a camera. They made a movie of this sneeze and called it *Record of a Sneeze*.

The first movies did not have sound. Radio had become so popular in 1925 that people stopped going to movies. In 1927 the first film with sound was made. It was called *The Jazz Singer* and starred Al Jolson. He spoke only a few lines, and there were a few songs, but people loved it. Putting sound and movies together was here to stay.

58

1. Underline the cause, and circle the effect.
   A. Dickson made a movie projector. He wanted a lot of people to see a movie at the same time.
   B. Dickson liked the idea of moving pictures. He filmed his first movie, *Monkey Shines*.
   C. Ott sneezed in front of a camera. It was made into a movie.
   D. Because of the radio, people stopped going to movies.

2. Crossword Puzzle

   Across
   4. When this came out, people quit going to movies.
   6. last name of the person who helped invent movies

   Down
   1. A movie is made of moving _____.
   2. The first movies didn't have any of this.
   3. made of twenty-four pictures per second
   5. the first word in Dickson's movie title

   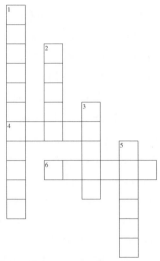

3. Number the events in the order that they happened.
   A. ___ Edison helped make the first movies.
   B. ___ One movie was called *Monkey Shines*.
   C. ___ Once a photograph is taken, it is put together with other pictures.
   D. ___ The kinetoscope was a box with a small hole in it.

4. Bonus Word Play
   Homophones are words that have the same sound but are spelled differently. Find the right homophone for each word.
   maid _____   sew _____   inn _____

The History of Hopscotch

The game of hopscotch began in ancient Britain. Back then, Britain was part of the Roman Empire. Hopscotch courts were 100 feet long, and they were used to train soldiers. Roman soldiers ran the length of the hopscotch course wearing their armor and packs. They did this to increase their strength and improve their footwork. Police officers and football players do things like this today.

The children of the Roman soldiers started drawing their own small courts. They liked to pretend they were soldiers. They also added points to their courts so they could keep score. Soon hopscotch spread all through Europe.

The word *London* is often written at the top of a hopscotch game. This comes from the Great North Road, which Roman soldiers used. The road was 400 miles long and led from London to the north.

Children all over the world play hopscotch. Hopscotch is also called "hop-around," "paradise," or "airplane," even though the game is played the same. In France, children draw the hopscotch court in the shape of a snail. They call the game escargot. *Escargot* is French for "snail." Children in Denmark throw heavy, glass markers onto their hopscotch courts.

There are many different ways to play hopscotch. In one of them, you put a marker between your feet. Then you have to hop from square to square without dropping it.

1. Write *T* for true or *F* for false in the blank next to each sentence.

A. ___ The game of hopscotch began in ancient Rome.

B. ___ The children liked to pretend they were kings and queens.

C. ___ Soldiers played hopscotch to improve their footwork.

D. ___ Hopscotch is also called "hop-a-long."

2. Fill in the blank with the right word from the story.

A. The game of hopscotch began in ancient _____.

B. In France, the hopscotch court is drawn in the shape of a _____.

C. The word _____ is often written at the top of a hopscotch game.

D. Hopscotch courts used to be _____ feet long.

3. Match the sentence with the correct answer in the box.

A. The Great North Road was _____ long.

B. In Denmark, markers are made of _____.

C. Hopscotch used to be used to train _____.

D. Hopscotch is also called _____.

1. glass
2. 400 miles
3. soldiers
4. paradise

4. Bonus Word Play

How many syllables are in each word?

soldiers _____

escargot _____

ancient _____

The Incredible Dead Sea

The lowest place on Earth (except the ocean) is called the Dead Sea. This strange lake is located in the Middle East, near Jerusalem. Israel is located on one side of the sea. The country of Jordan is on the other. The sea is 49 miles long and 10 miles wide. The waters are saltier than the ocean. This is why anybody can float in it.

The sea is full of minerals. The minerals collect here because the Dead Sea has no outlet. Calcium, sulfur, and potassium chloride are just some of the 21 minerals found in the Dead Sea. Many of these minerals have important uses. For example, potassium chloride is used to make fertilizer. Because of all the salts and minerals, fish cannot live in the water. This is one reason why it is called the Dead Sea.

The sun shines nearly every day of the year. The humidity is low, and the air is clean and free of pollen. This is good for people with allergies. Because the sea is so low, the air pressure is high. It has eight percent more oxygen than air anywhere else on Earth. This makes it easier to breathe. Plus, constant evaporation fills the air with healthy minerals

Many people think the sea and its climate are relaxing. The black mud along the shore is filled with minerals that cleanse the skin, relax muscles, improve blood circulation, and relieve pain. You can find many hotels and spas along the Dead Sea. This strange sea has become a popular place to go on vacation. Some people call it the largest natural spa in the world.

1. Write *F* for fact or *O* for opinion in the blank next to each sentence.
   A. ___ The lowest place on Earth (except the ocean) is the Dead Sea.
   B. ___ The Dead Sea would be fun to visit.
   C. ___ Potassium is an ingredient found in fertilizer.
   D. ___ Marine life and fish cannot live in these waters.

2. Answer the following questions.
   A. How are the Dead Sea and the ocean different?

   _____

   _____

   B. What can anyone do in the Dead Sea? _____

   C. What makes the air at the Dead Sea different from anywhere else on Earth? _____

   D. What do the 21 minerals have in common?

   _____

   _____

3. Circle the correct answer.
   A. The largest natural spa in the world is _____.
      the Red Sea   the Pacific Ocean   the Dead Sea

   B. Minerals are found along the shore in _____.
      buckets   the black mud   the morning

   C. The minerals of the Dead Sea are good for _____.
      your skin   the ocean   trees

   D. Air with no pollen is good for people who suffer from

      _____.
      the chicken pox   allergies   anger

4. Bonus Word Play
   Unscramble the following word: S L A R E N I M

   _____

The art of bringing drawings to life on a screen is called animation. Animation started in 1828 when Paul Roget invented the *thaumatrope*. The thaumatrope was a disc with a string attached to it. On one side Roget put a picture of a bird. On the other side he put a picture of a cage. When Roget twirled the disc, the bird looked like it was in the cage.

To make an animated movie, artists start by making hundreds of drawings. Each drawing is changed a little. When they are linked together and filmed one after another, the characters look like they are moving.

One of the earliest animators was Winsor McCay. He is best known for his film *Gertie the Dinosaur*. This was made in 1914.

When the first films were made, each person or place was drawn one by one. This was very hard to do because it took hundreds of drawings to make one minute of film. Then someone figured out how to keep the background the same, but the people's actions had to be drawn separately. Computers were finally invented that made animation a lot easier because computers could copy the pictures instead of people having to draw them by hand.

Walt Disney is well known for his animated films because he was the first person to put sound to animated movies. His first movie, *Steamboat Willie*, was made in 1928. In 1937 he made the first full-length animated movie, *Snow White and the Seven Dwarfs*.

Reading Comprehension

1. Underline the cause, and circle the effect.

    A. Paul Roget helped discover animation by inventing the thaumatrope.

    B. When the hundreds of pictures are filmed, they look like a steady flow of movement.

    C. *Snow White* was popular because it was the first full-length animated movie.

    D. One of the earliest animators was Winsor McCay. He is best know for *Gertie the Dinosaur*.

2. Crossword Puzzle

Across

2. first name of one of the earliest animators

4. last name of person who invented the thaumatrope

5. another word for *connected*

Down

1. series of drawings linked together

2. first name of person who made *Snow White*

3. Animation is a series of these.

3. Number the events in the order that they were told.

    A. ___ One of the earliest animators was Winsor McCay.

    B. ___ Walt Disney's first movie was *Steamboat Willie*.

    C. ___ Paul Roget invented the thaumatrope.

    D. ___ Hundreds of drawings make up one minute of film.

4. Bonus Word Play

Antonyms are words that have the opposite meaning. Find the antonym in the story for each of the following words:

after _____   different _____   easy _____

The United States Mint

Did you ever wonder where that quarter in your pocket came from? In the United States, coins are made at the United States Mint. The first U.S. Mint was built in Philadelphia in 1793. To make coins, the Mint must follow strict rules and have people watch over every step.

The word *mint* comes from the Latin word *moneta. Moneta* means *coins.* In 269 B.C., the Romans built a mint near the temple of Juno Moneta, where they made silver coins.

After the Constitution was signed, the Mint was the first building the new United States government built. George Washington chose David Rittenhouse to be the first director of the U.S. Mint. Some people say George Washington gave some of his own silver to the Mint. Thomas Jefferson designed our money system, which is based on units of ten. Before the Mint, different colonies produced their own coins. People also used wampum, farm goods, and even animals to pay for things.

At one time, the idea of making doughnut-shaped coins at the Mint was considered, but small, round coins were finally decided upon. Each coin is a different size because each is worth a different amount.

From 1864 to 1873, the Mint made a two-cent coin. This coin was the first to include the words "In God We Trust." The first Lincoln penny was made in 1909.

Reading Comprehension

```
      ¹r
       i
       t               ²w
       t                a
³j  e  f  f  e  r  s  o  n                      ⁴m
       n                h                        i
       h        ⁵p  h  i  l  a  d  e  ⁶l  p  h  i  a
       o                n               i         n
       u                g               n         t
       s                t               c
       e                o              ⁷m  o  n  e  t  a
                        n               l
                                        n
```

1. Write questions for the crossword answers.

   Across

   3. _____

   5. _____

   7. _____

   Down

   1. _____

   2. _____

   4. _____

   6. _____

2. Design your own coin. What would be on the front? What would be on the back? Why? How much would it be worth?

The Ferris Wheel

Do you think a Ferris wheel looks like a merry-go-round on its side? There is a good reason. The man who invented the Ferris wheel got the idea by watching a merry-go-round. George Ferris wondered if a merry-go-round could do the same thing if it was turned on its side. He got so excited about this idea that he drew it on a napkin one night while he was eating dinner.

George Ferris was a bridge builder. He knew a lot about making strong bridges. He used this knowledge to make the Ferris wheel strong enough to hold people in chairs while going around and around.

The first Ferris wheel was built in 1893. It was just in time for the Chicago World's Fair. The fair celebrated Christopher Columbus's coming to America four hundred years earlier. The people who planned the fair wanted something that would make this World's Fair something people would never forget. George Ferris helped them reach this goal.

The Ferris wheel stood 264 feet tall and had 36 chairs. It could hold 60 people. Tickets cost 50 cents each. The ride was so popular that it made $726,805.50 during the World's Fair.

That Ferris wheel was taken down in 1906, but Ferris wheels are still popular. You can still find them at theme parks and carnivals today.

Reading Comprehension

Word Bank		
bridge	Chicago World's Fair	George
60	side	1906
	excited	

1. Complete the chart with the words from the box.

The first name of the man who invented the Ferris wheel

was _____. He was a _____ builder. He was

_____ about his idea of putting a merry-go-round on

its _____ and seeing if it would go around and around. He

built the Ferris wheel for the _____ _____

_____. The Ferris wheel could hold _____

people. The Chicago Ferris wheel was taken down in

_____.

2. Now use five of these words in sentences of your own.

A. _____

B. _____

C. _____

D. _____

E. _____

The State Department

The world has over 190 countries. This is like having over 190 different neighbors. We share the world with all these neighbors. We work with them, and we buy and sell each other's goods. Sometimes we disagree as well. Because of all these things, it is important that we talk with the people in other countries. Talking helps us understand each other. This helps our country stay safe.

The president picks a group of people to talk to people in other countries. These people work for the government. The place where they work is called the State Department. The State Department began on September 15, 1789. Thomas Jefferson was its first leader.

The person in charge of the State Department is the secretary of state. The secretary of state oversees 5,000 employees. He or she is fourth in line to become president of the United States if something happens to the president. The secretary of state gives the president advice on problems with other countries and travels to other countries to represent the United States. The secretary of state is also in charge of all United States *ambassadors*. An ambassador represents the United States in a different country.

If you are planning a trip to another country, you'll need a passport from the State Department. The State Department also gives visas to people who want to visit the U.S.

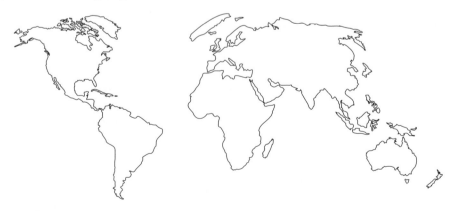

Reading Comprehension

1. In which encyclopedia volume would you find information on the following:
   A. secretary of state

   Sec – See   Sta – Sto   Sea – Seb

   B. Thomas Jefferson

   Jee – Jeg   Thi – Tho   Tha – Thi

   C. ambassador

   Ala – Ama   Amm – Amo   Amb – Amc

2. What are some of the things the State Department does?

   _____

   _____

   _____

3. Is having a State Department a good idea? _____

   _____

   _____

   _____

   Why? _____

   _____

   _____

4. How does the State Department help you feel safe?

   _____

   _____

   _____

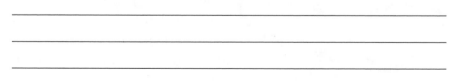

71

Ice Cream, You Scream

You can thank Marco Polo for one of America's favorite desserts: ice cream. Marco Polo saw ice cream made in China. He thought ice cream was such a good idea that he brought it back to Italy.

Ice cream was first served in the United States in the 1700s. Governor Bladen of Maryland gave it to his guests at a party. America's first ice cream parlor opened in New York City in 1776.

Dolley Madison was the first person to serve ice cream at the White House. She was the wife of President James Madison. A new president usually has a party called an *inaugural ball*. Dolley Madison served ice cream at James Madison's inaugural ball. After that, ice cream was served often at the White House.

In 1846 Nancy Johnson invented the first hand-cranked ice cream machine. She was a housewife from New England. Her machine made ice cream–making a lot easier, and the ice cream was a lot smoother.

The ice cream cone was invented at the World's Fair in St. Louis, Missouri, in 1904. Ernest A. Hamwi was selling a waffle pastry. The people in the booth next to him were selling ice cream. When they ran out of dishes, Hamwi rolled up his pastries and sold them to the ice cream booth. They put ice cream in them and sold ice cream cones.

Americans eat about 15 quarts of ice cream per person per year.

Reading Comprehension

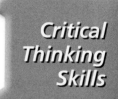

What Happens Next?

1. What did Marco Polo do after he discovered ice cream?

    _____

    _____

2. What happened to ice cream after Nancy Johnson invented her ice cream machine?

    _____

    _____

3. When the booth next to him ran out of dishes, what did Ernest A. Hamwi do?

    _____

    _____

4. On Your Own
    Invent a flavor of ice cream. What will you call it? What will you put in it?

73

Answer Pages

Page 3
1. **A.** O   **B.** F   **C.** F   **D.** O
2. **A.** D   **B.** D   **C.** D   **D.** D
3. **A.** Yellowstone Park **B.** window
   C. bushes   **D.** food
4. see, their, ate

Page 5
1. **A.** Four hundred people carved the
   mountain. Millions visit Mount
   Rushmore each year.
   B. Dynamite was used. Four hundred
   fifty thousand tons of granite were
   removed.
   C. Gutzon Borglum passed away. His
   son finished the job for him.
   D. Special tools were used. Each face is
   as smooth as a sidewalk.
2.

3. **A.** 4   **B.** 1   **C.** 2   **D.** 3
4. 2, 3, 3

Page 7
1. **A.** F   **B.** F   **C.** T   **D.** T
2. **A.** harpston   **B.** Super Bowl
   C. pastimes   **D.** archery
3. **A.** 3   **B.** 1   **C.** 4   **D.** 2
4. millions

Page 9
1. **A.** F   **B.** O   **C.** O   **D.** F
2. **A.** S   **B.** S   **C.** D   **D.** S
3. **A.** generous **B.** warm **C.** good
4. opened, on, top, warm

Page 11
1. **A.** The first crew didn't enter the space
   station. The hatch was broken.
   B. The second crew died. A valve was
   broken.
   C. The men were too weak to stand.
   Exercise equipment was put on the
   next space station.
   D. The *Mir* could be resupplied. One
   man lived on *Mir* for 438 days.
2.

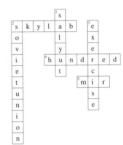

3. **A.** 1   **B.** 4   **C.** 3   **D.** 2

Page 13
1. **A.** F   **B.** T   **C.** F   **D.** F
2. **A.** D-Mart   **B.** rain
   C. baseballs **D.** FUN
3. **A.** 2   **B.** 3   **C.** 4   **D.** 1
4. tossed, bad, old

Page 15
1. **A.** F   **B.** O   **C.** O   **D.** F
2. **A.** temperature **B.** hands
   C. protective **D.** spots
3. **A.** Asia **B.** 15 seconds
   C. males **D.** a burglar alarm

Page 17
1. **A.** I am the president of my club. I have
   to clean my room.
   B. I am wondering some things. Could
   you please answer my questions?
   C. If you need help, call me.
   D. Someone told me you have a dog.
   Please say hi to your dog.

74

Answer Pages

2.

```
    ¹a      ²p
  ³f  o  u  r  t  h
    r      e
    a      ⁴s  i  n  ⁵k
    i      d      e
    d      ⁶c  l  u  b
           e      s
           n      y
           t
```

3. A. 2   **B.** 3   **C.** 1   **D.** 4
4. be, know, hi

Page 19
1. A. F   **B.** T   **C.** T   **D.** F
2. A. rain   **B.** bottom
   C. dents   **D.** thunderstorm
3. A. 2   **B.** 3   **C.** 4   **D.** 1
4. 2, 4, 1

Page 21
1. A. F   **B.** O   **C.** F   **D.** F
2. A. S   **B.** D   **C.** S   **D.** D
3. A. birthday   **B.** ringmaster
   C. show   **C.** horses
4. announces

Page 23
1. A. John Montagu could not eat with both hands. So he ordered a meal he could eat with one hand.
   B. Other people ordered sandwiches because they were hungry too.
   C. Elizabeth Leslie put the sandwich recipe in a cookbook. Americans learned how to make them.
   D. Sliced bread was invented. The sandwich became even more popular.

2.

```
  ¹b
²r  e  ³c  i  p  e
  e     a
  a     r     ⁴m
  d     d     o
        ⁵s  a  n  d  w  i  c  h
              t
              a
              g
        ⁶f  o  u  r  t  h
```

3. A. 4   **B.** 2   **C.** 1   **D.** 3

Page 25
1. A. F   **B.** T   **C.** F   **D.** F
2. A. jazz   **B.** May
   C. "Good job."   **D.** fourth
3. A. 4   **B.** 3   **C.** 1   **D.** 2
4.

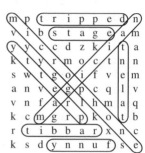

Page 27
1. A. F   **B.** O   **C.** F   **D.** F
2. A. S   **B.** D   **C.** D   **D.** S
3. A. fairies   **B.** cheers   **C.** tame   **D.** sew
4. A. cheers   **B.** teach   **C.** pretty

Page 29
1. A. When people didn't listen to him play the piano. Mozart started to cry.
   B. His father played the violin. He taught Mozart how to play it too.
   C. Mozart became a concertmaster. He wasn't paid well.
   D. Mozart was a happy boy. People liked him.

2.

```
                    ¹c
                    o
              ²f    m
  ³m  o  z  a  r  t    p
              t        o
              ⁴a       s
        ⁵r  e  q  u  i  e  m
              r        r
              s
              t
              r
        ⁶f  i  v  e
              a
```

3. A. 4   **B.** 2   **C.** 1   **D.** 3

75

Answer Pages

Page 31
1. A. F   **B.** T   **C.** T   **D.** F
2. A. Theodor Seuss Geisel
  B. Massachusetts
  C. pen   **D.** *The Cat in the Hat*
3. A. 2   **B.** 3   **C.** 1   **D.** 4
4. A. one   **B.** write   **C.** night

Page 33
1. A. F   **B.** O   **C.** F   **D.** O
2. A. chair   **B.** sick
  C. safety bar   **D.** counted
3. A. screamed
  B. Kim wants to ride the roller coaster,
    but Megan doesn't.
  C. a big, mean, mechanical dragon
  D. The ride up the hill was slow. The ride
    down the hill was fast.

Page 35
1. A. Crocodiles eat rocks. Rocks help
    them stay underwater.
  B. To help it stay cool, a crocodile opens
    its mouth.
  C. Mother crocodiles need to protect
    their young. They carry their babies in
    their mouths.
  D. Crocodiles watch other animals. Then
    they know when to catch them.
2.

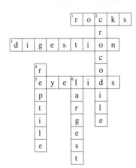

3. A. 3   **B.** 4   **C.** 2   **D.** 1
4. fifteen

Page 37
1. A. F   **B.** T   **C.** F   **D.** T
2. A. Rover   **B.** birthday party
  C. Casey   **D.** Mary
3. A. 2   **B.** 3   **C.** 4   **D.** 1
4. A. opened **B.** filled   **C.** underneath

Page 39
1. A. O   **B.** F   **C.** F   **D.** O
2. A. S   **B.** D   **C.** S   **D.** D
3. A. zap   **B.** neutrons
  C. attract each other **D.** positive energy
4.

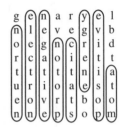

Page 41
1. A. Louisa loved writing. She became
    famous.
  B. Louisa went to work. She became a
    seamstress.
  C. *The Inheritance* was found after
    Louisa died. It was published.
  4. She wrote *Flower Fables.* She wanted
    to entertain Emerson's daughter.
2.

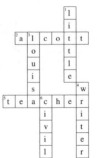

3. A. 4   **B.** 1   **C.** 3   **4.** 2

76

Answer Pages

Page 43
1. **A.** F   **B.** F   **C.** F   **D.** F
2. **A.** hide   **B.** chemicals
   C. glowworms   **D.** one
3. **A.** 3   **B.** 1   **C.** 2   **D.** 4
4. **A.** a flying insect   **B.** shines at night
   C. an insect

Page 45
1. **A.** F   **B.** O   **C.** O   **D.** O
2. **A.** Sarah has a broken leg.
   B. Both Carmen and Sarah have diaries.
   C. Carmen is older than Billy.
   D. Carmen has the chicken pox.
3. **A.** her hand was getting tired
   B. homework   **C.** secrets
   D. bored

Page 47
1. **A.** The Little Newshan was built. (People) (didn't carry buckets of water to a fire)
   B. If people passed buckets of water to the fire. (the fire could be put out.)
   C. So the horses would not get hurt, (they wore special shirts.)
   D. Sirens were put on fire trucks. (Bells) (were no longer used.)
2.

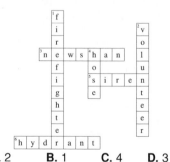

3. **A.** 2   **B.** 1   **C.** 4   **D.** 3
4. **A.** 3   **B.** 3   **C.** 1

Page 49
1. **A.** F   **B.** T   **C.** T   **D.** F
2. **A.** Sardis   **B.** smart
   C. 200   **D.** Greece, 620 B.C.
3. **A.** 3   **B.** 4   **C.** 1   **D.** 2
4. Aesop

Page 51
1. **A.** O   **B.** F   **C.** O   **D.** F
2. **A.** S   **B.** D   **C.** D   **D.** S
3. **A.** fell asleep   **B.** kept going
   C. starting line   **D.** race
4. **A.** slow   **B.** always   **C.** wrong

Page 53
1. **A.** Annie looked out the car window. (She) (saw a sign on a telephone pole)
   B. (Everyone said no when Annie) asked if anyone had seen a small, black dog.
   C. (Annie's family missed their dog) when they lost her.
   D. Tom knocked on the door. (A tiny old) (lady answered.)
2.

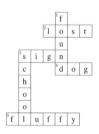

3. **A.** 4   **B.** 1   **C.** 2   **D.** 3

Page 55
1. **A.** F   **B.** T   **C.** T   **D.** F
2. **A.** Salesmen   **B.** 23
   C. Fleer   **D.** artificial
3. **A.** 4   **B.** 3   **C.** 1   **D.** 2
4. **A.** sticky   **B.** hoped   **C.** invented

Page 57
1. **A.** F   **B.** O   **C.** O   **D.** F
2. **A.** eggs   **B.** toast
   C. pajamas   **D.** brothers
3. **A.** cupboard   **B.** a yellow paper
   C. gone   **D.** ate their mother's breakfast

Answer Pages

Page 59
1. **A.** Dickson wanted to make a movie projector. He wanted a lot of people to see a movie at the same time.
   B. Dickson liked the idea of moving pictures. He filmed his first movie, *Monkey Shines.*
   C. Ott sneezed in front of a camera. It was made into a movie.
   D. Because of the radio, people stopped going to movies.
2.

3. **A.** 2   **B.** 4   **C.** 1   **D.** 3
4. **A.** made   **B.** so   **C.** in

Page 61
1. **A.** F   **B.** F   **C.** T   **D.** F
2. **A.** Britain   **B.** snail   **C.** London   **D.** 100
3. **A.** 2   **B.** 1   **C.** 3   **D.** 4
4. **A.** 2   **B.** 3   **C.** 2

Page 63
1. **A.** F   **B.** O   **C.** F   **D.** F
2. **A.** The Dead Sea is saltier than the ocean.
   B. float
   C. The air has eight percent more oxygen.
   D. Many have important uses.
3. **A.** the Dead Sea   **B.** the black mud
   C. your skin   **D.** allergies
4. minerals

Page 65
1. **A.** Paul Roget helped discover animation by inventing the thaumatrope.
   B. When hundreds of pictures are filmed, they look like… flow of movement.
   C. *Snow White* was popular because it was the first… animated movie .
   D. One of the earliest animators is Winsor McCay. He is best known for *Gertie the Dinosaur*.

2.

3. **A.** 2   **B.** 4   **C.** 1   **D.** 3
4. **A.** before   **B.** same   **C.** hard

Page 67
1. Answers will vary.
   (7) another word for *coin*
   (3) designed our money system
   (2) gave some of his own silver
   (4) a place where coins are made
   (5) where the first Mint was built
   (6) the face on a penny
   (1) first director of the U.S. Mint
2. Answers will vary.

Page 69
1. The first name of the man who invented the Ferris wheel is <u>George</u>. He was a <u>bridge</u> builder. He was <u>excited</u> about his idea of putting a merry-go-round on its <u>side</u> and seeing if it would go around and around. He built the Ferris wheel for the <u>Chicago</u> <u>World's</u> <u>Fair</u>. The Ferris wheel could hold <u>60</u> people. The Chicago Ferris wheel was taken down in <u>1906</u>.
2. Answers will vary.

Page 71
1. **A.** Sec–See   **B.** Jee–Jeg
   C. Amb–Amc
2–4. Answers will vary.

Page 73
1. He brought it back to Italy.
2. It became easier to make, and the ice cream was smoother.
3. He rolled up his waffles and sold them to the ice cream maker, who sold them as cones.
4. Answers will vary.

78